PERFORMANCE EDITIONS

BEETHOVEN
TWO SHORT SONATAS
Opus 49

Edited and Recorded by Robert Taub

T0071563

To access companion recorded performances online, visit:
www.halleonard.com/mylibrary

Enter Code
4726-1166-4245-9662

On the cover:
River Valley Landscape
by Caspar David Friedrich
(1824-1825)

© Alexander Burkatovski/CORBIS

ISBN: 978-1-4234-2724-7

G. SCHIRMER, Inc.

DISTRIBUTED BY
HAL•LEONARD®
CORPORATION
7777 W. BLUEMOUND RD. P.O. BOX 13819 MILWAUKEE, WI 53213

www.musicsalesclassical.com
www.halleonard.com

CONTENTS

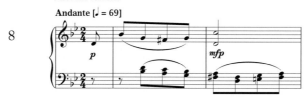

HISTORICAL NOTES

LUDWIG VAN BEETHOVEN (1770-1827)

THE PIANO SONATAS

In 1816, Beethoven wrote to his friend and admirer Carl Czerny: "You must forgive a composer who would rather hear his work just as he had written it, however beautifully you played it otherwise." Having lost patience with Czerny's excessive interpolations in the piano part of a performance of Beethoven's *Quintet for Piano and Winds*, Op. 16, Beethoven also addressed the envelope sarcastically to "Herr von Zerni, celebrated virtuoso." On all levels, Beethoven meant what he wrote.

As a composer who bridged the gulf between court and private patronage on one hand (the world of Bach, Handel, Haydn, and Mozart) and on the other hand earning a living based substantially on sales of printed works and/or public performances (the world of Brahms), Beethoven was one of the first composers to became almost obsessively concerned with the accuracy of his published scores. He often bemoaned the seeming unending streams of mistakes. "Fehler—fehler!—Sie sind selbst ein einziger Fehler" ("Mistakes—mistakes!—You yourselves are a unique mistake") he wrote to the august publishing firm of Breitkopf und Härtel in 1811.

It is not surprising, therefore, that toward the end of his life Beethoven twice (1822 and again in 1825) begged his publishers C.F. Peters and Schott to bring out a comprehensive complete edition of his works over which Beethoven himself would have editorial control, and would thus be able to ensure accuracy in all dimensions—notes, pedaling and fingering, expressive notations (dynamics, slurs), and articulations, and even movement headings. This never happened.

Beethoven was also obsessive about his musical sketches that he kept with him throughout his mature life. Desk sketchbooks, pocket sketchbooks: thousands of pages reveal his innermost compositional musings, his labored processes of creativity, the ideas that he abandoned, and the many others—often jumbled together—that he crafted through dint of extraordinary determination, single-minded purpose, and the inspiration of genius into works that endure all exigencies of time and place. In the autograph scores that Beethoven then sent on to publishers, further layers of the creative processes abound. But even these scores might not be the final word in a particular work; there are instances in which Beethoven made textual changes, additions, or deletions by way of letters to publishers, corrections to proofs, and/or post-publication changes to first editions.

We can appreciate the unique qualities of the Beethoven piano sonatas on many different levels. Beethoven's own relationship with these works was fundamentally different from his relationship to his works of other genres. The early sonatas served as vehicles for the young Beethoven as both composer and pianist forging his path in Vienna, the musical capital of Europe at that time. Throughout his compositional lifetime, even when he no longer performed publicly as a pianist, Beethoven used his 32 piano sonatas as crucibles for all manner of musical ideas, many of which he later re-crafted—often in a distilled or more rarefied manner—in the 16 string quartets and the nine symphonies.

The pianoforte was evolving at an enormous rate during the last years of the 18th century extending through first several decades of the 19th. As a leading pianist and musical figure of his day, Beethoven was in the vanguard of this technological development. He was not content to confine his often explosive playing to the smaller sonorous capabilities of the instruments he had on hand; similarly, his compositions demanded more from the pianofortes of the day—greater depth of sonority, more subtle levels of keyboard finesse and control, increased registral range. These sonatas themselves pushed forward further development and technical innovation from the piano manufacturers.

Motivating many of the sonatas are elements of extraordinary—even revolutionary—musical experimentation extending into domains of form, harmonic development, use of the instrument, and demands placed upon the performer, the piano, and the audience. However, the evolution of these works is not a simple straight line.

I believe that the usual chronological groupings of "early," "middle," and "late" are too superficial for Beethoven's piano sonatas. Since he composed more piano sonatas than substantial works of any other single genre (except songs) and the period of composition of the piano sonatas extends virtually throughout Beethoven's entire creative life, I prefer chronological groupings derived from more specific biographical and stylistic considerations. I delve into greater depth on this and other aspects of the Sonatas in my book *Playing the Beethoven Piano Sonatas* (Amadeus Press).

1795-1800: Sonatas Op. 2 no. 1, Op. 2 no. 2, Op. 2 no. 3, Op. 7, Op. 10 no. 1, Op. 10 no. 2, Op. 10 no. 3, Op. 13, Op. 14 no. 1, Op. 14 no. 2, Op. 22, Op. 49 no. 1, Op. 49 no. 2

1800-1802: Sonatas Op. 27 no. 1, Op. 27 no. 2, Op. 28, Op. 31 no. 1, Op. 31 no. 2, Op. 31 no. 3

1804: Sonatas Op. 53, Op. 54, Op. 57

1809: Sonatas Op. 78, Op. 79, Op. 81a

1816-1822: Sonatas Op. 90, Op. 101, Op. 106, Op. 109, Op. 110, Op. 111

From 1804 (post-Heiligenstadt) forward, there were no more multiple sonata opus numbers; each work was assigned its own opus. Beethoven no longer played in public, and his relationship with the sonatas changed subtly.

—Robert Taub

PERFORMANCE NOTES

For the preparation of this edition, I have consulted autograph scores, first editions, and sketchbooks whenever possible. (Complete autograph scores of only 12 of the piano sonatas—plus the autograph of only the first movement of Sonata Op. 81a—have survived.) I have also read Beethoven's letters with particular attention to his many remarks concerning performances of his day and the lists of specific changes/corrections that he sent to publishers. We all know—as did Beethoven—that musical notation is imperfect, but it is the closest representation that we have of the artistic ideal of a composer. We strive to represent that ideal as thoroughly and accurately as possible.

General Observations

Tempo

My recordings of these sonatas are included in the published volume. I have also included my suggestions for tempo (metronome markings) for each sonata, at the beginning of each movement.

Fingering

I have added my own fingering suggestions, all of which are aimed at creating meaningful musical constructs. As a general guide, I believe in minimizing hand motions as much as possible, and therefore many of my fingering suggestions are based on the pianist's hands proceeding in a straight line as long as musically viable and physically practicable. I also believe that the pianist can develop senses of tactile feeling for specific musical patterns.

Pedaling

Beethoven did not include pedal markings for these sonatas. However, whenever necessary one should use the right pedal—sparingly and subtly—to help achieve legato playing as well as to enhance sonorities.

Ornamentation

My suggestions regarding ornamental turns concern the notion of keeping the contour smooth while providing an expressive musical gesture with an increased sense of forward direction. The actual starting note of a turn depends on the specific context: if it is preceded by the same note (as in Sonata Op. 10 no. 2, second movement, m. 42), then I would suggest that the turn is four notes, starting on the upper neighbor: upper neighbor, main note, lower neighbor, main note.

Sonata in F Major, Op. 10 no. 2:
second movement, m. 42, r.h.

However, if the turn is preceded by another note (as in Sonata Op. 10 no. 2, first movement, m. 38), then the turn could be five notes in total, starting on the main note: main note, upper neighbor, main note, lower neighbor, main note.

Sonata in F Major, Op. 10 no. 2:
first movement, m. 38, r.h.

Whenever Beethoven included an afterbeat (Nachschlag) for a trill, I have included it as well. When he did not, I have not added any.

About the Edition

Footnotes within the musical score offer contextual explanations and alternatives based on earlier representations of the music (first editions, autograph scores) that Beethoven had seen and corrected. In specific cases that are visible only in the autograph score, I explain the reasons and context for my choices of musical representation. Other footnotes are intended to clarify ways of playing specific ornaments.

Above all, Beethoven's sonatas—as individual works, or taken together as a complete cycle—are pieces that we can listen to, learn, play, put away, re-learn, and perform again over and over—with only increasing joy, involvement, and meaning. For those of you looking at the musical score as you follow a recording, welcome. For those playing these pieces for the first time, I invite you to become involved. And for those returning to these sonatas after learning them previously—or comparing this edition to any other—I invite you to roll up your sleeves and start playing, for there is always more to do.

The expressive universe conjured up by the Beethoven piano sonatas is unprecedented, and unequalled.

Notes on the Sonatas*

The two Sonatas Opus 49 are both small pieces of two movements; their very intimacy is their greatest challenge to the performer. Their brevity, the succinct qualities of their themes, their limited registral range and scale of dynamics—all are smaller in scope than those of any sonata that Beethoven had composed previously (including even the three very early ones, WoO 47, that Beethoven did not publish). Yet they are impeccably crafted and demand pianistic control, particularly finesse in voicing and dynamics.

*Excerpted from *Playing the Beethoven Piano Sonatas* by Robert Taub
© 2002 by Robert Taub
Published by Amadeus Press
Used by permission.

Sonata in G minor, Opus 49 no. 1 (1798)
First Movement: Andante

The first sonata is the more somber of the two. The pacing of the first movement, in G minor, is gentle and ambling (Andante); the sobriety of character can easily be weakened by playing too fast. At the very beginning of the piece, I make a distinct dynamic differentiation between the songful, plaintive melody and the accompanying chords, but nevertheless voice the left-hand legato chords slightly to the top. The 16th-note accompanying figures in the second theme are then softer, more in the background, which helps to enhance the contrast in texture and character between the first and second themes. The loudest sustained part of the short first movement is the *forte* opening of the development area with the trills in both hands, but this fades back to *piano* by the fourth measure, the cadence on E-flat major. Although no dynamic is indicated, I make a subtle crescendo in mm. 62-63.

Sonata in G minor, Op. 49 no. 1:
first movement, mm. 61-63

Tension builds in these measures as the right hand ascends chromatically, preparing—as we hear retrospectively—for the main theme to reenter as a surprise, *piano subito*, in m. 64. I take a bit of time at the beginning of the last eight-bar phrase—the coda—as B-natural is introduced (m. 103) to change from G minor to G major. But tempo primo is resumed almost right away and the piece ends quietly, in tempo, without a ritard, leaving us hanging, waiting for the next movement.

Second Movement: Rondo: Allegro

The ensuing Rondo: Allegro is lively, but the pulse is six eighth-notes to the bar, not in two, and the tempo is determined by the speed of the 16th-notes, not the eighth-notes. The opening theme is confined to the middle register, as is the first theme of the Andante, and the weighting implied by the slur over the B–G is a subtle way of showing the change in character from the minor interval B-flat–G of the first movement. The light character of the Rondo's opening becomes slightly more intense with the second theme, which is back in G minor and includes crescendos to *forte*. Clear portrayal of mood among the alternating themes in this Rondo is among the most important aspects of the piece, particularly since the themes are so concise. In the area of greatest profusion of dynamic indications (beginning in m. 135) the motivic unit of the main theme is tossed playfully back and forth between the two hands in different registers before the coda concludes with the theme safely back in the right hand and two *fortissimo* cadential chords.

Sonata in G Major, Opus 49 no. 2 (1796)
First Movement: Allegro, ma non troppo

Sonata Op. 49 no. 2 provides a challenging opportunity to consider one's understanding of Beethoven's early compositional and performing style, for there are no dynamic markings whatsoever in the first edition (Bureau d'Arts et d'Industrie, 1805). Modern editions are based on this first edition since the autograph has been lost, and any dynamic markings are simply editorial. In performance, therefore, to judge appropriate dynamics, one applies one's own understanding of Beethoven's style of this era, of how he integrated the musical elements: tempo, character of themes, harmonic and metrical relations, nature of pianism. I begin the opening of Sonata Op. 49 no. 2 with feelings of confidence, aplomb, and a touch of bravura, *forte*. Rather than dropping to *piano* in m. 2 with the start of the slur (as is the case in some editions), I prefer to carry on in *forte* until the phrase winds down in m. 4, at which point I make a slight decrescendo, only to begin the repeat of the theme *forte* again. The quiet and more registrally confined second theme, which begins at the end of m. 20, can be *piano* until m. 36, which is again more brilliant. The development also begins *forte*, but then I drop immediately to *piano* for the triplet in the second half of m. 53. This contributes to feelings of surprise and anticipation, for the mode is minor for the first time and there is some question as to where the music is leading. Aside from the next *forte* motivic half-note (m. 56)—which is now in A minor—I like to maintain the level of *piano* for the remainder of the development, but the arrival of the main theme back in G major is *forte*.

Second Movement: Tempo di Menuetto

The second movement is marked Tempo di Menuetto. The only other piano sonata movement Beethoven marked similarly is the first movement of Sonata Op. 54. The minuet theme is the basis for the theme of a similar movement (Tempo di Menuetto) in the *Septet for Winds*, Op. 20. The theme in the piano sonata is basically *piano* and the two contrasting episodes are *piano* and *forte* respectively. The ways in which each episode leads back to areas of the main theme are simple, elegant, and balanced: the first via the right hand, and the second via the left.

Sonata in G Major, Op. 49 no. 2:
second movement, mm. 44-48

Sonata in G Major, Op. 49 no. 2:
second movement, mm. 85-88

The coda, beginning in mm. 107-108, introduces rests into the dotted figure of the main theme which, as the line descends, make it feel both more airy and more resigned. One could build drama with a crescendo as the line then ascends, but I think it is most in keeping with the intimate, impeccably crafted nature of these two "brother" works to end the last chords softly, foregoing any temptation toward a more brilliant *forte* ending.

—Robert Taub

Sonata in G minor

Ludwig van Beethoven
Opus 49 no. 1

*without tail (ohne Nachschlag)

Rondo
Allegro [♩. = 92]

Sonata in G Major

I

Ludwig van Beethoven
Opus 49 no. 2

Allegro, ma non troppo [♩ = 76]

*There are no dynamic markings included in the first edition (Kunst und Industrie-Comptoir, Vienna, 1805). All dynamic markings in this sonata are suggestions of the current editor.

*without tail (ohne Nachschlag)

Tempo di Menuetto [♩ = 100]

ABOUT THE EDITOR

ROBERT TAUB

From New York's Carnegie Hall to Hong Kong's Cultural Centre to Germany's *avant garde* Zentrum für Kunst und Medientechnologie, Robert Taub is acclaimed internationally. He has performed as soloist with the MET Orchestra in Carnegie Hall, the Boston Symphony Orchestra, BBC Philharmonic, The Philadelphia Orchestra, San Francisco Symphony, Los Angeles Philharmonic, Montreal Symphony, Munich Philharmonic, Orchestra of St. Luke's, Hong Kong Philharmonic, Singapore Symphony, and others.

Robert Taub has performed solo recitals on the Great Performers Series at New York's Lincoln Center and other major series worldwide. He has been featured in international festivals, including the Saratoga Festival, the Lichfield Festival in England, San Francisco's Midsummer Mozart Festival, the Geneva International Summer Festival, among others.

Following the conclusion of his highly celebrated New York series of Beethoven Piano Sonatas, Taub completed a sold-out Beethoven cycle in London at Hampton Court Palace. His recordings of the complete Beethoven Piano Sonatas have been praised throughout the world for their insight, freshness, and emotional involvement. In addition to performing, Robert Taub is an eloquent spokesman for music, giving frequent engaging and informal lectures and pre-concert talks. His book on Beethoven—*Playing the Beethoven Piano Sonatas*—has been published internationally by Amadeus Press.

Taub was featured in a 2003 PBS television program—*Big Ideas*—that highlighted him playing and discussing Beethoven Piano Sonatas. Filmed during his time as Artist-in-Residence at the Institute for Advanced Study, this program has been broadcast throughout the US on PBS affiliates.

Robert Taub's performances are frequently broadcast on radio networks around the world, including the NPR (Performance Today), Ireland's RTE, and Hong Kong's RTHK. He has also recorded the Sonatas of Scriabin and works of Beethoven, Schumann, Liszt, and Babbitt for Harmonia Mundi, several of which have been selected as "critic's favorites" by *Gramophone*, *Newsweek*, *The New York Times*, *The Washington Post*, *Ovation*, and *Fanfare*.

Robert Taub is involved with contemporary music as well as the established literature, premiering piano concertos by Milton Babbitt (MET Orchestra, James Levine) and Mel Powell (Los Angeles Philharmonic), and making the first recordings of the Persichetti Piano Concerto (Philadelphia Orchestra, Charles Dutoit) and Sessions Piano Concerto. He has premiered six works of Milton Babbitt (solo piano, chamber music, Second Piano Concerto). Taub has also collaborated with several 21st-century composers, including Jonathan Dawe (USA), David Bessell (UK), and Ludger Brümmer (Germany) performing their works in America and Europe.

Taub is a Phi Beta Kappa graduate of Princeton where he was a University Scholar. As a Danforth Fellow he completed his doctoral degree at The Juilliard School where he received the highest award in piano. Taub has served as Artist-in-Residence at Harvard University, at UC Davis, as well as at the Institute for Advanced Study. He has led music forums at Oxford and Cambridge Universities and The Juilliard School. Taub has also been Visiting Professor at Princeton University and at Kingston University (UK).